What To Do

When You Don't Know What To Do

Women uplifting women through stories of victory

Author

Tendai Jordan

2016

Copyright © 2016 Tendai Jordan

All rights reserved.

ISBN:-10 0692697551

DEDICATION

This book is dedicated to my powerful granddaughter Cha Olivia and all the powerful women who know what to do.

CONTENTS

Acknowledgments

Introduction

		Page
1	Keep Going - Elise LeBec	8
2	The Mundane Parts of Life – Abena Otudor	11
3	Find the Positive – Kim Olver	15
4	Let Go – Tendai Jordan	23
5	What to do Next – Judith Rich	30

APPENDICES

A	What Others have Said	38
B	Suggestions on What to Do	42
C	Your 'What to do' Exercise	46

ACKNOWLEDGMENTS

A thousand times thank you to my powerful sister and best friend Cheryl, who has been with me in all the important ways from the beginning.

I am so grateful for the women, Elise, Abena, Kim, Judith and Tanya who had enough faith in me to say 'yes' to contributing to this work.

And so much appreciation to Powerful Women International Connections (PWIC) for supporting me and encouraging me to get this out.

INTRODUCTION

I want to say up front that the intention of this eBook, entitled, "*What To Do When You Don't Know What to Do,*" is to uplift the reader, offer solutions and most importantly to encourage a shift in your thinking. The wonderful contributing authors are people like you and me who have opened up their hearts and shared with us their experiences when they felt like they didn't know what to do and how they dealt with it.

BACKDROP

As I was trying to decide on what the topic of this book should be, many ideas came to mind, so much so that the whole idea "sat on the shelf" for a few more days.

I continued to work on other tasks I had pending, some overdue according to my own time table, and wondering "what should I be working on next? What is the important step?" I allowed myself to become "stuck." Yes, I had a plan, I had a vision, I set my intentions, but I just didn't know what to do next.

It seemed like I had too many options. Should I work on my book; what can I do for my website; how about posting on Facebook, or should I just get out of the house? When all of these thoughts were going through my head, I just stopped. I tried to identify the feeling and I knew it was not "overwhelm." I felt more like a hamster on the never ending wheel, or I was having a "Ground Hog Day" experience. I know that the best start to addressing the situation is to begin with the right questions. Questions that will lead to a resolution and not a "woe is me," feeling. My questions to myself were: "What is this experience teaching me," and "Who can I talk to for assistance?"

Then a question came to me, <u>what do you do when you just don't know what to do</u>? "Hey, maybe that can be the title of my book." "And maybe, just maybe, other people have had the same or similar experience and like me just couldn't move forward with any confidence."

I then decided to ask powerful women to contribute to this work. Some of them I knew directly and some I knew only by reputation. I felt all of them could contribute some insight to this dilemma.

I made a list of powerful, talented, women, but I found the asking part was a little intimidating for me. Ahhhh, yet something else I'll have to deal with, by spending time going within myself. I know I have the skill and experience for making a list, getting the contact information and even determining how to contact them in this age of Internet, Facebook, Twitter and the like. Sometimes the simple phone call just wasn't an option. No problem, research, I got this. So now that I had the contact information, the confidence waned and those negative thoughts showed up; "what do I say," "what if they say, no," "can I really do this," you are not important enough;" Ooohh the thoughts kept coming and the project sat a little longer as I worked through the fear and confidence issues. Well, I worked through the resistance, contacted several beautiful women, and got several affirmatives and a few "can't do it" responses. I was thrilled just to get the responses and that as they say "is history." I consider this project a successful endeavor.

The powerful women who stepped up and said, "YES" to contributing the chapters that follow, seemed to go deep within themselves and share a time when the "don't know what to do," feeling came up for them and it was accompanied or initiated by pain. But through reading their experiences you begin to identify a common theme, which is more than I expected.

After reading the thoughtful contributions I was inspired to take a closer look at those times I had the experience and then I decided to write a chapter myself. As I was writing my own chapter on the topic, some new insights were revealed to me as to what causes this "don't know what to do" feeling and what the subsequent actions should be. I have noticed of late that when I get an idea or message to do something it comes like an onion. It seems like a good idea, it even seems simple enough to carry out given my experience and skills. But what I have become very aware of is how in the implementation of the idea, the layers of the onion begin to peel away and I begin to experience other thoughts. Feelings come up that lead to a deeper understanding of who I am.

So here we are, for those of us who meditate, pray, develop a plan, identify your mission, state your intentions, build your vision boards, are open and available and one day just don't know what to do next, whether it's about your business, your relationships, your kids, your jobs, your travels or all of the above, here are, prayerfully, some key tips from others and <u>what they did, when they didn't know what to do.</u>

In the appendices, I have added some exercises and other pieces after the chapters to assist the reader in addressing their own experience on the topic.

1. A List of Empowering Questions
2. What Others Have Said
3. Suggestions on What To Do
4. 'What To Do' Exercise

My intention as stated previously is that you, the reader,

will not only enjoy the book, but if you experience a situation of not knowing what to do that you will move with a new consciousness <u>knowing that</u> you do know what to do.

Keep Going

By Elise LeBec

When I was six years old my parents decided to get a divorce and so my father took custody of me and my mother took my three-year-old sister. This was my first experience of not being in control and not knowing what to do or how to do it. It was very hard for me to understand why I could not live with my mother and why my parents did not want to live together anymore.

I think this experience has shaped all other experiences in my life because of the way I react when I don't know what to do. I find that waiting, taking the time to reflect and not move seems to be one of the ways I cope with the mystery of "not knowing".

Often times I have become angry or impatient, pushing things to happen even when I wasn't sure that was the correct direction. This has sometimes worked in my favor, making things come together through my intuition rather than logical thinking. At other times this has ruined opportunities for myself and pushed people away. I can say that more than often when I didn't know how to do something it came to me rather quickly with movement. Sometimes, just creating movement can help focus direction and lead you to a more "knowing" place.

As a child I had big dreams. Never for a second did I think

that I didn't know how to make my dreams happen. I certainly did not know at the time what to do but something inside of me assured me that all would be revealed in time. This has been the majority of my experience. When I turned 18 I travelled the world living in places like, London, New Zealand, Australia. I was there because I wanted to be there. I had dreamed of travelling the world, I never knew how I would get there, but I hung onto this dream and one day woke up to find myself living my dream.

Intention and movement are the keys to making things happen when you don't know how. My intention to travel led me to buy a ticket I couldn't afford when I was 18 to fly to England. A weird thing happened, right before I went to England I met a man who was from there but who happened to be living in the USA at the time. We met through my employer and he fell madly in love with me. It took me three months to realize that we were meant to be together. It was his dream to travel the world as well and he had the money to do it. Soon after I got back from England, we left the USA and ended up travelling the world together for the following six years.

When I turned 20, I decided that I wanted to be a professional composer. I had no idea how to do that and the very thought of it used to make me twitch with nervousness. I wanted it so badly but felt that I was so far away from ever becoming good enough. So, I kept going. I kept practicing, kept moving in the direction of where I wanted to be. It was hard, I was impatient but I kept going no matter how hard it got and it did get hard. There were moments when I had no money, no inspiration and no idea of what to do next. I just kept going toward my goal and eventually ten years later in 2006, I released my first piano album called "Possible Dreams" Impressions of a Solo Piano. This album went straight to number 12 on the new age radio charts and is still selling digitally today bringing in a decent amount of money and inspiring its listeners. All of this came about because I didn't know what to do, but I kept going anyway.

If there is one thing I would like to say to anyone who may be afraid to start something because they don't know how to do it, I would say, "You never know how to do something until you start doing it. Therefore you should start as soon as possible while time is on your side. Even the biggest, the richest, the most successful people in the world would lament that they don't know what they are doing half the time, they just keep going in the direction of their goal and somehow, some way, it all gets done. It's like magic!

Elise is an experienced Composer, talented Pianist and consummate Entrepreneur. She has always been willing to share her gift and works with other musicians to assist them in achieving their dreams. You can learn more about this fabulous woman by visiting her website: http://www.eliselebec.com

Mundane Parts of Life

By Abena Otudor

"Ready for the Revolution" is how he would answer the phone whenever I was lucky enough to catch him on the other end of the line. Many knew him as Kwame Ture; some knew him as Stokely Carmichael in the days when he marched alongside of such civil rights, human rights and revolutionaries as Dr. Martin Luther King, Jr., Willie "Mukassa" Ricks, Andrew Young, Jesse Jackson and the like. I simply knew him as Brother Kwame. He was indeed a mentor for me. Through the years I grew to respect his courage for standing up for truth, and his love and compassion for Afrikan people and many others around the globe.

Over many years we would cross paths in different community meetings. I was also instrumental in organizing numerous speaking engagements for him, in which he delivered challenging and inspiring messages from the organization he represented. There were several times that my husband and I had the honor of hosting him in our home when he visited the area to do his work.

I got the news of his passing as I was getting ready for work. It happened quite by accident. Ordinarily any pertinent news I receive from sources other than the TV or radio. But this day I heard his name. I don't often listen to the news and to hear his name on mainstream radio was a surprise. I thought it was odd, but it got my attention. So I stopped and listened very intently to the newscaster giving sketchy details of Brother Kwame making his transition while he was in Guinea, West Africa. He had succumbed to prostate cancer.

A picture I had seen of him in Jet magazine months earlier flashed in my head. It showed him in a hospital in Guinea as Jesse Jackson stood by his side. He was very tall, well over 6 feet. In the picture, he had lost a lot of weight and appeared very frail. But as was characteristic of him he gathered his strength and posed for the picture, and I smiled at the warrior gleam in his eye. It said, as I had felt from him before and heard him say in so many speeches, "victory is certain!"

Snapping out of the memory back to what I had just heard on the radio, I sunk down to the carpet and let out a wail from the deepest part of my soul. The tears flowed for at least 10 minutes as I debated whether or not to go to work that day. I instantly went from happy go lucky starting my day to being grief ridden to hear that someone I had laughed and talked with and admired had passed. I had never given up hope that he would recover. To hear it in that fashion I was not prepared and it struck me like a hail of bullets. I even had to stop to make sure I was hearing it correctly.

Then the questions started pouring into my mind, "I am hurting right now, what do I do?" "Do I go to work feeling grief all day?" "Should I just suck it up and not show the grief?" "Do I act like nothing has happened?" I didn't know what to do. I know I needed to have a good cry. I was also going through a divorce and having spent a lot of time crying I now had one more thing to grieve about. So I decided to let the tears flow until I was able to make a decision.

I picked myself up and began to pace the floor as tears turned to sniffles. I didn't know just what to do, what could I do? I remember feeling helpless for a moment and wondering who could I call and where could I go, since I was no longer an active member of the same organization.

I went to the bathroom, looked in the mirror at my reddened, damp eyes.

After letting go and releasing the pain, I was able to make a decision. I decided to go into work and carry on my responsibility. The mundane parts of life still had to go on. I felt like I was in a daze or trance, but I got ready and went to work. I wasn't myself and just going through the motions. I felt like it was the right thing to do. I had the strength to carry on.

I was sad and quiet the whole day thinking how the world would not be the same without this magnificent warrior actively engaged in battle somewhere on this big planet of ours. That this mighty giant of a man had taken the time to talk to me, to write me, to ask how my family was doing during his visits was quite humbling to me as well as inspirational and powerful at the same time.

Days later, I showed up late for the memorial service, again due to the mundane things of life taking front seat. I was prepared to deal with the grief this time. My purse was full of tissues. Yet, to my surprise I found other brother and sister warriors there celebrating his life and beating the drums, literally, speaking to his life and his many contributions to the forward movement of our people the world over. "No tissues necessary for this celebration!!!"

Looking back now, it appears odd and yet very much in perfect order how the focus on mundane, yet very necessary, parts of life moved me through this time of pain. I didn't know what to do but, I did it anyway. My interactions with Kwame and experiencing the pain of his passing, yet the celebration of his life gave me the inner strength to move when I didn't know what to do or say. It has contributed to the strong woman I am on this very day.

Abena lives in Atlanta, Georgia and facilitates the African Women's Sacred Healing Circle. Her interest is for women to have the courage to heal themselves. She can be reached by email: Womansacred7@yahoo.com. Her message to you is: I am a sister with a quiet strength and determination and humbled by people that think so much of me. I love you."

Find the Positive

By Kim Olver

When I was asked to contribute a chapter to this book about a time in my life when I didn't know what to do, the biggest challenge of my life came to mind.

When I was away at college, my parents' 20-year marriage was disintegrating. I wasn't there to see it every day but when I would come home for the holidays, I noticed my father wasn't home a lot. He was going to bars drinking and my youngest brother, age 14, was really giving my mother a hard time. She would tell him he couldn't do something and he would do it anyway.

I remember saying, "Please God, whatever you do, don't let me be a single mother raising teenage boys by myself!" After watching my brother interact with my mother, I came to believe that boys only respected physical strength. By the time they were teenagers, they realized they were stronger than their mothers and so could do whatever they wanted.

A few years later, I got married myself. Then over time, I gave birth to two sons. They were the light of my life. I loved those boys with everything I had and in balance, my husband disciplined them with everything he had. I was the pushover mom, often giving in to their whims and my husband was the one who held them accountable and made them tow the mark.

In a perfect world, we would have both demonstrated an equal amount of support and discipline however, in our home, I was the supportive one and my husband was the disciplinarian. It may not have been the best system but as long as we were a unit, we did provide equal parts. It's just that almost all the support came from me and almost all the challenge came from my husband. Things worked fairly well.

Then one day early in 1995, my husband was diagnosed with leukemia. The doctors were very optimistic. My husband was young (33), he was very healthy other than the leukemia, and he had six brothers and sisters willing and able to be his bone marrow donor.

During this time, I knew what to do. My job was to be supportive and optimistic. At this time, my children were ten and eight years-old. I did my best to keep everything as normal as possible for them.

When it came to my husband, I knew I had to keep working. He stopped working when he realized a chemical he worked with in his job, Benzene, was linked as a cause to his type of leukemia. It was the health insurance plan through my job that was going to pay for his expensive bone marrow transplant. I had to keep working, so work I did.

His brothers and sisters were all tested to see if they were matches but none of the six were. Our children were not a match and neither of his parents was a match.

My husband and I went to work with an entire community of family, friends and absolute strangers to raise money to get more people registered as bone marrow donors. We raised enough money to add 800 new names to the bone marrow registry. Still I knew what to do . . . support and optimism.

I convinced my husband to take a trip with me and our boys to Florida and Disney World so we would have positive memories, just in case.

In January 1999, four years from his original diagnosis, we traveled from Northeast Pennsylvania to Milwaukee, WI to Froedtert Hospital, known at the time to have the greatest success with mismatched donors, which is what my husband had.

My first moment of indecision occurred when we had to decide if we would take our boys with us or leave them home. At this point, one was in 7th grade and the other in 9th. They had a strong network of support between family and friends and it was the middle of wrestling season, a sport with which my children were very involved. What was a mother to do? This could be the last months they would have to spend with their father, but was it right to uproot them and take them away from everything familiar?

I had no idea what to do, so I asked them. They opted to stay in PA with their grandmother but it was possible for them to also make frequent brief trips to Milwaukee as their schedules allowed. I made some trips back to PA, as well. It seemed a reasonable compromise.

Then on June 22, 1999 the unthinkable happened. My husband, my parenting partner, died. Now I **really** didn't know what to do. Nothing could have prepared me for this. The only people I ever knew who had died were old! My husband was only 37 years-old.

How would I help my children grieve? How would I hold things together for his mother, brothers and sisters? How would I ever raise teenage boys by myself? It was my biggest nightmare!

What to do? Who knew? I had to figure it out. I knew I wasn't going to shrivel up and die too. I had two children depending on me.

I began to think about what I already knew that could help me with this situation, and who I knew who might be able to teach me whatever else I needed to know.

I was an instructor for The William Glasser Institute, teaching Choice Theory to audiences all over the world. I believed in Choice Theory and basically lived my life according to its tenants.

The first thing I needed to do was to get a handle on my grief so I could help my children with theirs. I had read a book, *The Breakthrough Experience*, and believed what author, John Demartini, said about all things having equal positive and negative value attached to them. I intimately knew the negative side of my husband's death but how could I find the positive?

But I was motivated. I wanted to be able to help my children, especially my youngest son, who was having a particularly difficult time. When I thought about it, I was able to find two positive things. First of all, because my husband had a long-term illness, everyone who had a relationship with him had the opportunity to say goodbye. We left no words unsaid. Our last words to him were loving. There were no regrets.

The second positive thing was the way my husband lived the last four and a half years of his life. Prior to his diagnosis, my husband was a workaholic. He left at seven in the morning and returned around nine each night. He worked Saturdays and on Sundays he would work on his own cars (he was a mechanic). My children and I didn't get much quality time with him. However, once he learned about Benzene possibly causing his leukemia, he stopped working. He wasn't so sick he couldn't work, but he was attempting to minimize his risk.

He chose to spend his time with our children. He coached their soccer and Little League teams. He mentored them in wrestling and took them to many private tournaments. He took them hunting and fishing and genuinely spent more time with them in those four and a half years than he would have had he lived to be 100 and healthy!

Once we were able to find those positives, things got a little better for all of us. As time went on, we found others. It definitely got us through the rough spots.

I had heard other parents, mostly divorced parents who felt they were parenting alone, say, "I had to be mother and father to my kids." That never made sense to me. I don't think a mother can be a father to her children. I never tried to father mine. However, I knew they were missing a male influence in their lives. I reached out to men I trusted to spend time with them—family friends, uncles, a grandfather, and male teachers and coaches at school.

There was a gap I was not able to fill but I could find appropriate people to help my children get their need met for a male role model. It definitely wasn't the same as having their father in their lives, but they had some wonderful men who invested their time in helping them figure out how to become men. For that, I will always be grateful. I didn't know what to do or how to do it, but I did know people who could and would.

I still had the challenge of raising my kids without the disciplinarian. I had no experience with this. I knew how to support them. I didn't know how to say no. I didn't know how to get them to do the things I wanted them to do. I didn't know how to help them become responsible.

Or did I? Again, I decided to rely on what I knew best—Choice Theory. I had worked 15 years for a specialized foster care agency helping foster parents raise other people's children who had special needs. I knew a whole lot about parenting traumatized children. I just had never applied those ideas to my children. I had been so busy balancing my husband out, just as he had been simultaneously balancing me out.

I knew applying Choice Theory to my parenting would provide the balance of support and discipline my children needed but it was unchartered territory. I didn't know what to do. I asked myself the question, "Who do I know who can help me with this?"

I knew I couldn't count on people in my family or my husband's family. They did not understand Choice Theory. They thought I was too permissive with my children. The only person I could think of who would be able to help me do what I wanted to do was a woman living in Rhode Island, Dr. Nancy Buck. Dr. Buck had been my first instructor in Choice Theory and she had written a book about parenting based on those concepts.

When I didn't know what to do, I found someone who had already been successful at what I was trying to do. I hired her to be my parenting coach while I was going through the teenage years with my children. And remember, I wasn't just going through normal teenage things. I had all that plus the grief of the boys losing their father. Dr. Buck helped me stay the Choice Theory course.

What does that mean? Well, I had to be aware of what my own needs were and get them met. I had to be aware of my sons' needs and help them learn how to meet them in a responsible way. I had to be clear in my expectations, and know how to talk to my kids when they broke the rules and did things that weren't responsible.

It meant focusing on teaching them instead of punishing them. They got to do the things they wanted to do as long as I was convinced they had the responsible behaviors to stay safe in the situation.

I won't say it was a walk in the park. Actually, it was hard work and there were great moments of joy. Sometimes we fought. My children and I stayed connected and talked through some challenging situations. We trusted each other.

Today they are 25 and 27 years-old. Both are married and each of them has their own son now. I couldn't be a prouder parent and grandparent and now I know exactly what to do. All I have to do is love them. And I am giving back by teaching Choice Theory parenting to other parents who just don't know what to do.

Coach, Speaker & Author of Leveraging Diversity at Work & Secrets of Happy Couples, Kim believes "All great relationships begin and end with yourself" She can be found at Kim@therelationshipcenter.biz and www.KimOlver.com

Let Go

By Tendai Jordan

I am happy to explore this topic and share the insights that I gleaned from the experiences over the years in which I felt like I didn't know what to do. I "got skills" and some experience so when things happen, I don't get thrown into a doo loop very easily.

As I was remembering the times I was in the throes of not knowing what to do, it was not about what restaurant to eat at or what to wear to a party, I am talking about those times when the "to do something" is important and the not knowing is causing gut wrenching pain and stark fear of the "what is going to happen to my life if I don't do something?" There are those times when I am stopped in my tracks without a clue as to "what to do next."

When I examine some instances where this happened in the past, I think it's important to look at the feelings around them, not only the circumstances themselves, in order to describe what I mean. I asked myself, "What was going on?" There are those times, when things seem to be sailing along, moving smoothly and then all of that stops and things aren't going as "I" had planned. The situation takes a turn and the plan is no longer working.

One significant time is when I was out of a job and months had gone by. Months of looking on the Internet, monster.com and all the other job searching sites. I had been down the list of "how to get a job" and done the networking, talking to friends, even a few exploratory interviews, yet I still didn't have a job. The money was getting very funny lookin' and I didn't know what to do, or where to go.

Another time that comes to mind, is when several years ago, my husband and I were not able to get along. I thought the love was still there, but the efforts toward better communication and understanding seemed to go out the door. I read books about relationships. I tried talking and explaining, and sharing. I talked to my minister. I prayed. I tried being quiet. I even cooked dinner as if that would solve the problem and yet nothing really changed. When I was finally able to talk him into counseling and that went awry, I found myself having the same feelings of powerlessness and hopelessness. I didn't know what to do.

What really stands out for me is raising my daughter as a single parent.

Now, I had support and help. Although her father was living across country, he was available by phone. But, in my mind that was not viable, significant support; because, the day to day decisions and steps to be taken seemed to all fall on me. As I mentioned before I 'm no wimp, I don't just lay down when times get a little rough, but raising a child is serious business. I had all of the same ideas, dreams and plans as most parents. I wanted my daughter to be safe, happy etc. But sometimes I couldn't make that happen. There were instances when something happened and I felt it was on me to do or say something and I didn't know the "right" thing to do or say.

Even now as I write this chapter, I think back over the last few years and how my life has taken some twists and turns and I find myself on a new path of creating, developing, building, and starting my own business. Now I'm a business woman. Six years ago this wasn't even an option I would have considered for my life. But like I said, "twists and turns," and here I am. I didn't just jump into something, I am a baby boomer so you know I did the research and talked to people and went to seminars, and read books, even sought out the SBA etc. But you better believe that there was more than one occasion that I got to a step in the plan and it was not working, even after following all of the directions of the famous "gurus." Several times I found myself saying, "What the hell do I do now?" What is wrong with this picture?

If you resonate with any of this or experienced similar situations, just stay with me here.

So, through meditation and taking a posture of allowing, I began to not only reflect on the past instances of this happening, but to examine what is really going on with me during these stressful times of not knowing what to do and that is where this chapter really begins to open up and share for everyone.

In order to address this situation in a way that supports me and others in a real way I took a look at it by first asking empowering questions.

- What is going on?

- What am I feeling?

- How is the feeling manifesting in my body?

- What is the Spirit trying to tell me?

- How can I perceive this situation, first from the inner me?

These questions guided me to take a good look at the situation and allow the answers or solutions to be revealed to me. Is this how it goes for you? Things are moving along smoothly, you are doing your work, living your life, following directions, doing the "right" thing. Then, they are not, according to your expectations. Ahhhh so *expectations* are part of the equation. The outcome of your plan is different than expected. And it is not "a good one" Or the rent is due today and the miracle hasn't happened yet. OK, sooooo.. *time* is a factor in this equation. Things don't happen when you want them to or think they should. When your young daughter is crying, your husband of 11 years walks out, the clients are not coming to your new business or the money is short and the rent is due and the emotions come up with the negative thoughts. *Victim-ness* raises its ugly head. Why is this happening to me? Why can't I be successful like so and so? Why doesn't what I do work? What's wrong with me? So I dare to say there is that *ego* involved. I have no control. Uh-ohhh there's that evil big "C" -*control* revealing itself. The overall feeling is powerlessness. And for a recovering control freak like me, that is a biggie.

So now the question comes, "what do you do when you feel powerless?" When you feel alone and I dare say afraid; when your heart is heavy and your stomach is in knots? Once you identify and recognize the real issue, it is easier to resolve or address.

LET IT GO. By "it" I mean the attachment to the situation, let go of the emotion and thinking you can control the outcome. Once I looked at the past situations and identified the feelings, I have learned to relinquish the idea that I am in control. I stopped thinking that I have to do anything or that something has to be done right now. So when the "what to do" feeling comes I am much better prepared. And, yes, sometimes I have to remind myself over and over, every day, until a new feeling comes. Be still, relax and you'll know what to do.

I was watching the TV program Discovery about the 9/11

attacks on the World Trade Center and what has been happening up to now, leading into the 10th Anniversary of the Twin Towers collapsing. The program discussed not only the devastation and the deaths and the impact on the people who were working in the Towers at the time, but also the local businesses and homes of people around the area. They arrived home to see 2-3 feet of dust, and ash, body parts and debris inside their apartments. People were looking at their homes and all that stuff and wondering "what do we do now?"

What about the Katrina storm, and bomb attacks on a country that leave the local grocery stores and hospitals gone and schools closed, with children on the streets. And think about the earthquake in Haiti, then the storms and the fighting in the Middle East and Africa. These things cause people's lives to be devastated. Talk about a big change. I cannot even imagine what that initial feeling is, "what the hell do I (we) do now?" But that's a different book for another time.

I believe that the time we don't feel like we know what to do is just a moment in time. Sometimes it feels like hours or days or even years, but it's only a moment. It's that time that Iyanla Vanzant calls "in the meantime." It's that time that Terry McMillan calls "waiting to exhale." As soon as we release and we can exhale, then the meantime value is revealed and we know what to do, because it was there all the time. It was just blocked by our need to control, inappropriate expectations and feeling disconnected from our Source.

As my above-stated situations unfolded I knew what to do. The action follows the thought and the thought is clear; keep doing what you're doing, up the ante, and ask the empowering questions. It required me to forgive myself or anyone I had blamed.

I dare say that what brought me to the point of feeling like I didn't know what to do and then the subsequent action all had to do with my own consciousness.

I am grateful for Spirit guiding me to explore this issue. The whole process of getting this together and dealing with my feelings has really helped me to know what to do if the feeling comes again. I have to get out of my own way, let go and allow myself to be guided to right action.

Tendai is a teacher, life enhancement coach and facilitator. She is Founder and Creator of take One Night Off A Week aka tONOAW, a program that encourages you to go deep within so you can live full out. You can get more information on http://TendaiJordan.com and TendaiJordan1@gmail.com.

What to Do Next?

By Judith Rich

The topic what to do when you don't know what to do is very timely and important, especially now, when we humans are facing change at such an extraordinary level and pace. We're often left overwhelmed, not knowing what to do next.

When I query people in the personal development seminars I lead about their purpose for attending, a majority of participants respond with some variation on the following:

I feel lost.
I don't have a direction for my life.
I just got laid off. How do I start over?
I know where I want to go. I just don't know how to get there.
I know what I don't want, but I don't know what I do want.
I don't even know where to begin.

Sound familiar? Join the club. It turns out this is territory many of us know well. Most people are first faced with this "what do I do with myself now" challenge in their early to mid twenties, as they enter adulthood and expect to begin careers. It used to be that after one finished high school, college or the military, one could expect to secure a good job and begin building a life. Forget about that today.

High school grads that can't afford to go to college have increasingly looked to the military to provide the next level of education and training to equip them with job skills. But the sustained economic crisis has changed everything. According to an article in the Washington Post, <u>unemployment among young vets</u> of the Iraq and Afghanistan wars hit 21.1 percent last year as many returned home to find their jobs had been eliminated due to downsizing while they were deployed.

Young adults, ages 18-24, are the hardest hit in this prolonged recession. <u>The Bureau of Labor Statistics</u> cites the unemployment rate at 18.3 percent among Caucasian men, 30.1 percent among Blacks and 20.1 percent among Hispanics in this age group. So clearly, there are a lot of folks who don't know what to do next, and there aren't a lot of open doors beckoning them to enter.

But this phenomenon is not reserved only for the young. Across a lifetime, nearly everyone reaches a place where, in order to go forward, letting go of what no longer serves or works and reinventing oneself anew is required. In fact, given the amount of rapid change characteristic of the times in which we live, men and women all across the age spectrum can expect to retool several times during a lifetime.

Sometimes it happens out of necessity, as in the current jobs crisis. Perhaps that career no longer has the promise it once had, due to companies downsizing or going out of business altogether. Many new college graduates find themselves with a degree in a field that now has little opportunity, and are happy to find anything just to survive.

Sometimes we find ourselves starting over because we've become disappointed or disillusioned in a career we thought was going to be a perfect match, only to discover that reality didn't match our expectations. Women who left a career to raise a family might now suddenly find themselves back in the job market because of divorce or just plain economic necessity.

Reaching retirement age is another stage of development where retooling becomes paramount. People used to think retirement meant sitting back, taking it easy, sleeping in late, and finally having the time to pursue those long lost dreams you left behind in the rat race of having to make a living.

Well, for many of today's retirees, that's also pretty much a myth. Many people of retirement age, having lost substantial life savings and investments in the stock market crisis, can no longer afford to retire, and perhaps have even lost their homes in the mortgage crisis. Furthermore, age discrimination in this jobless market is a major issue for people still needing to work and people are finding few opportunities available.

Some people are fortunate enough to have adequate financial resources and have the luxury of being able to choose when and if they want to stop working or to change careers midstream. Many say they know they don't want to keep doing what they've been doing, but they don't know what to do next.

But not all dilemmas of not knowing what to do next are necessarily career related. Relationships offer up another domain of big challenges in this area. People find themselves stuck in a marriage that long ago lost its luster, yet don't know how, or can't afford to, get out; or they don't have the skills to make it better. And sometimes, career and relationship challenges clash and then things really get intense.

In situations like these, what do you do when you don't know what to do?

It's human nature to want predictability. We're creatures of habit, seeking comfort and not well equipped to deal with the uncertainty that comes from finding ourselves at a dead end or in a cul-de-sac. We're not taught how to look beyond whatever is obscuring the path in front of us, or how to look within to find the inner resources necessary to grow larger than the obstacles we face. When faced with roadblocks that appear to be immovable, not knowing how to tap into our own resourcefulness, it's easy to get caught up in fear and anxiety, both of which are disempowering and render us even less capable of dealing with the crisis at hand.

Change doesn't come easily for most people, not because it is inherently difficult, but primarily because of what we tell ourselves about how difficult it's going to be. Reinventing oneself sounds like a big deal, and therefore it must be hard and require a lot of suffering. Right?

Not necessarily. Change requires suffering only if that's the conversation we're living inside. If we let fear choose for us, then we'll contract. In our misguided attempt to protect ourselves from what we've already decided is going to be painful, we armor ourselves by pulling back and being resistant to life as it's flowing in the moment. We're set up to suffer because that's the condition we've prepared for. And guess what? We'll be right. Suffering will be our experience. It's guaranteed.

Even under the most challenging of circumstances involving a great deal of pain and hardship, suffering is not required. There is a Zen aphorism that says, "Pain is inevitable; suffering is optional."

Consider the experience of Jose Rene "JR" Martinez, currently appearing as a contestant on "Dancing With The Stars." In 2003, JR, then with the U.S. Army in Iraq, was driving a Humvee whose left front tire hit a landmine. He suffered severe burns over 40 percent of his body, including his head and face. He spent the next 34 months in a military hospital recovering from 33 cosmetic surgeries and skin grafts to rebuild his face and badly burned body.

JR told his story publicly for the first time on a recent Monday night episode of DWTS. After his injuries, when he woke up in the hospital and asked to see his face in the mirror for the first time, he broke down and started crying. In the weeks that followed, he became severely depressed, filled with regrets and blame, and told himself it would have been better if he hadn't survived. He cried himself to sleep many nights. Then one day his mother was at his side as he was crying and she said something to him that changed everything. She told him that whoever was going to be in his life would be there because of who he was, not because of how he looked.

In that moment, something clicked inside JR and he understood he had a choice. He could go on being a victim and drown in his own self pity, or he could pick himself up and find a reason to go on. He chose the latter.

Talk about reinventing oneself. Since that fateful day when JR chose to make his life have new meaning, he's become a sought after motivational speaker. He travels all over the country speaking to veterans groups, non-profits, corporations and schools, bringing his message of resilience and optimism. In 2009, JR was honored by the Iraq and Afghanistan Veterans of America (IAVA) with the Veterans Leadership Award, given in recognition of his dedication to our newest generation of veterans.

But wait. There's more. JR has launched yet another career as an actor, being cast in the ABC Daytime drama, "All My

Children." He plays a character that was also injured in combat while serving in the military.

So getting back to our question: What do you do when you don't know what to do next? Just Be.

And I'm rooting for you to win whatever is there for you to claim and own as your own prize in this life. What you are seeking is seeking you.

What's worked for you to move on to the next stage of your life? What did you do when you didn't know what to do?

Judith Rich is a speaker, writer trainer, workshop facilitator and leadership development coach. Judith brings insight, passion, humor and sensitivity to empower people's awakening to the brilliance of who they are. She writes for the Huffington Post online. Her personal blog and website is, Rx For The Soul. She can be reached at: judith@judithrich.com.

APPENDICES

Appendix A

What Others Have Said

"You DO know what to do."

> *Louise Hay is an author of You Can Heal Your Life and also known as one of the founders of the self-help movement.*

"You never have to do anything. Don't know <u>what to do</u>? Do nothing. I wait. And that has been a big <u>lesson</u>: to be willing, to be still with myself, and <u>trust</u> myself and my higher power to help me make the right <u>decision</u>."

"I don't believe that anything happens without a reason. I don't believe it. And in order to believe 'That is the truth,' you have to believe it in all circumstances."

> *Oprah Winfrey, Journalist, talk show host, business woman and CEO of O Magazine and OWN TV*

"There is a scene in the movie "Back to the Future," where Marty McFly feels stymied by a problem. He feels there's no way around this problem and Doctor Brown says to him, "Marty, you're not thinking fourth dimensionally."

As soon as he begins to think fourth dimensionally, all of a sudden ideas come to him and then there's an answer provided. Thinking fourth dimensionally simply means thinking outside the problem. Instead of thinking how big the problem is, start thinking how big the universe is and then tell the problem how big the universe is."

"Ideas start to come to us when we realize we really have a capacity of thinking that gives us access to getting anything we choose. What will you choose this day? You have a day right now that you're holding that's yours to craft and shape and mold any way you choose. The day isn't contained by what's in it; it's contained by how you think about it. Let's think fourth dimensionally today. Here's To Today."

Mary Morrissey is a transformational speaker, the author of Building Your Field of Dreams, and No Less Than Greatness, a New Thought Minister, the President and Founder of "Life Solutions" and "Evolving Life Ministries". Mary is the Co-Founder and the first President to the Association for Global New Thought

"Inner silence promotes clarity of mind; It makes us value the inner world; It trains us to go inside to the source of peace and inspiration when we are faced with problems and challenges. Difficulties are opportunities toward better things; They are stepping stones to a greater experience."

> *Tanya Hanna lives in Nassau Bahamas. She is a musician and innovator, cofounder of You In Music, Prodigy Foundation, the author of Bahamian Musicians and Entertainers. Join her for dinner at Graycliff where she creates a relaxing atmosphere as she plays the piano and sings.*

"Even when you think you have your life all mapped out, things happen that shape your destiny in ways you might never have imagined."

> *Deepak Chopra is the author of more than sixty books translated into over eighty-five languages, including numerous New York Times bestsellers in both the fiction and nonfiction categories including The Seven Spiritual Laws of Success, and a Spiritual healer and leader.*

"You may encounter many defeats, but you must not be defeated. In fact, it may be necessary to encounter the defeats, so you can know who you are, what you can rise from, how you can still come out of it."

> *Maya Angelou is one of the most renowned and influential voices of our time. Hailed as a global renaissance woman, Dr. Angelou is a celebrated poet, memoirist, novelist, educator, dramatist, producer, actress, historian, filmmaker, and civil rights activist.*

"Your pain is the breaking of the shell that encloses your understanding."

> *Khalil Gibran, a poet, painter, philosopher and mystic - a writer who irrevocably changed modern Arabic poetry, and who is probably the one modern Arab writer known throughout the world.*

"As you begin to take action toward the fulfillment of your goals and dreams, you must realize that not every action will be perfect. Not every action will produce the desired result. Not every action will work. Making mistakes, getting it almost right, and experimenting to see what happens are all part of the process of eventually getting it right."

> *<u>Jack Canfield,</u> is best known as the co-creator of the <u>Chicken Soup for the Soul</u> book series, a motivational speaker and businessman and founder of the <u>Transformational Leadership Council</u>*

Appendix B

Suggestions on what to do when you don't know what to do:

First, just let it go for now. Don't do anything. Breathe. Ask yourself empowering questions.

Clarify your "story?" Become aware of what you're telling yourself about your current situation. Is this a "problem" or an "opportunity?" How you frame it will determine how you experience it. If you're having a "problem" chances are you're reacting from fear. If you choose to see this moment as an "opportunity," new possibilities and doors open. They were always there. You just weren't prepared to receive them.

Notice your body sensations. What is your body telling you right now? Is your throat tight? What about your stomach? Notice the sensations in your chest. And what about your breath? Is it shallow or deep? Slow or fast? The body has its own wisdom. It's rarely ever wrong. Learn to tune into it and trust it. It will tell you what to do, even if it's still. Become silent, and do nothing. Follow it.

Notice your feelings. Do you feel anxious, nervous, panicky or manic? Do you feel quiet, calm, and serene? Follow whatever you're feeling. Look at what lies beneath. And what's underneath that? Keep following your feelings.

You may have to go so deep into the feeling realm that the only way out is to go all the way through and out to the other side. This will sound counterintuitive at first. You mean to allow yourself to feel even more depressed? More sad? Yes, and when you do...

Ask for support. It's a good idea to have a trusted ally nearby. A therapist, a coach, a clergy member, a friend, a family member, someone who is skilled enough to help you hold this experience and support you to move through it. Remember, JR's mom was the catalyst that helped him moved beyond self-pity to making a conscious choice about how he wanted to live.

Get moving. Move your body: walk, run, dance, go to the gym, get a massage, do Pilates. Do whatever feels good and right for your body. Get those endorphins pumping, and you'll have a whole new perspective on what wants to happen next.

Trust the process. Know that you're in a process and that you're right where you need to be. How do I know? Because if you were supposed to be somewhere else, you'd be there. So give yourself permission to relax into it a bit and trust that even though you might not yet be able to see light at the end of this tunnel, you are making your way one step at a time. And on that note...

Be here now. Just take this one step at a time. You didn't get here overnight, so give yourself a break and allow the process to work on its own time. Yes, it's frustrating to feel stuck or lost and not know what's coming or which way to turn. The fog will settle when you're ready to see. Besides, the answers you seek aren't "out there." They're right where you already are. So look within, be still and know.

Open up. Open your eyes, ears, heart, mind, soul and life, to the possibility that something wonderful is being birthed in you right now, even if this moment is painful. Then remember #6.

Take a seat, and take a deep breath. And then another. The answers you seek lie in the breath. Breathe in love, acceptance, courage and peace. Breathe out fear. Developing a meditation practice where you simply observe the breath will allow the mind to clear and become focused.

Find something larger than yourself to serve. JR began by visiting his fellow burn patients in the hospital. His example gave them renewed hope. You have something worthwhile to give to others. Find those who need what you have to give, and then give. Know that what you are seeking is seeking you.

Add your suggestions

1.

2.

3.

4.

5.

Appendix C

Your "What to do" Exercise

1. <u>Identify</u>: the situation you are experiencing. Write it down and get it out.

2. <u>Clarify</u>: how you are feeling – what are the emotions you are experiencing?

3. <u>Identify</u>: the mind-body connection. Is the emotion showing up in your body anywhere? If so breathe through it. Focus energy to that area.

4. <u>Identify</u> your responsibility and discard the responsibility of any other person. You can't control anyone else. The focus is on you.

5. <u>Reflect:</u> Have you been in this situation before? Is this a pattern? What did you do? Did it work for you?

6. Ask yourself empowering questions? (Remember no "why" questions)

    <u>What</u> is this situation showing me? (about me)

    <u>What</u> can I learn from it?

Who can I talk to? (someone that will support your growth, uplift and hold accountable)

7. What is my next step?

www.ingramcontent.com/pod-product-compliance
Lightning Source LLC
Chambersburg PA
CBHW061300040426
42444CB00010B/2436